A SHORT GU
NUNHEAD CEMETERY

Tim & Carol Stevenson
(Editors)

F.O.N.C

Friends of Nunhead Cemetery - London

Abridged from *Nunhead Cemetery - An Illustrated Guide* first published 1988, reprinted with some amendments 1995.

Edited and abridged by Tim and Carol Stevenson from original articles by Chris Knowles, John Collings, Jeff Hart, Brent Elliott, Maggie Hart and Tim Stevenson.

The editors would also like to acknowledge the assistance of Gwyneth Stokes and Ron Woollacott in the preparation of this guide book.

Copyright © Friends of Nunhead Cemetery

First published in September 2003 and reprinted January 2006
This printing September 2008

Published by
The Friends of Nunhead Cemetery
c/o 185 Gordon Road.
LONDON
SE15 3RT

ISBN 0-9539194-5-5

Printed in Great Britain by Catford Print Centre, LONDON, SE6 2PN

CONTENTS

~~~~~~~~~~~~~~~~~~~~~~~~~

PREFACE

The Friends of Nunhead Cemetery published the very first comprehensive illustrated guidebook to the Nunhead Cemetery of All Saints in 1988; this was followed by a revised edition in 1995. Both editions were best-sellers and are now regrettably out of print.

Much has happened at Nunhead since the publication of the last edition, including the replacement of the boundary railings and the restoration of the historic core of the cemetery in the new millennium year, as a result of a welcome Heritage Lottery Fund grant of £1.25 million, and the upgrading of the cemetery, also in 2000, from Grade II to Grade II* (starred) in English Heritage's *National Register of Parks and Gardens of Historic Interest*.

This new concise guide, carefully edited and updated by husband and wife team, FONC committee member Tim Stevenson and vice-chairman Carol Stevenson, includes much useful and interesting information abridged from articles that appeared in the earlier guides, together with new and current information. This handy guidebook, therefore, is essential reading for all visitors to the historic and beautiful Nunhead Cemetery.

Ron Woollacott
FONC chairman

Maps: First time visitors may find the plan on the centre pages helpful (which can also be used with the suggested guide route). The smaller map on the inside back cover gives the burial square numbers, often needed for tracing graves.

HISTORICAL INTRODUCTION

Nunhead Cemetery is one of seven great Victorian cemeteries established in a ring around the outskirts of London. At the time the cemetery opened, Nunhead was a small hamlet surrounded by market gardens and open fields. Nunhead Hill, the site chosen for the cemetery, rises to two hundred feet above sea level at its highest point, and affords extensive views over the City of London and St Paul's in one direction, and towards the Downs in the other.

Within the City of London the population had expanded rapidly from around 900,000 in 1801 to 2,363,341 in 1851. The need for the decent and hygienic burial of the dead became an ever increasing problem. The traditional method was burial in a local churchyard, but these became so overcrowded that conditions were quite appalling.

The London Cemetery Company was established by Act of Parliament in 1836. It opened its first cemetery in 1839 at Highgate, and its second, All Saints at Nunhead, was opened for burials in 1840. Both Highgate and Nunhead continued to be managed by the London Cemetery Company and its successor companies until 1975.

The London Cemetery Company suffered from a major scandal in 1865 following the death of the company secretary, Mr Edward Buxton. It was discovered that he had been engaged in various frauds for many years, and he had embezzled a total of over £18,000 of the company's money - a vast amount in those days. He was buried at Nunhead, and his grave can still be seen. Despite this setback, the company recovered and flourished throughout the 19th century, resisting competition from the newer public cemeteries established after 1850, such as Camberwell Old Cemetery at Honor Oak.

After the First World War, the fortunes of the company began to decline. This was partly due to changing fashions, as people spent less on burials. Another factor was the ever increasing cost of maintenance and repairs.

In 1969, United Cemeteries decided that it could no longer

cope with the maintenance. They withdrew from the responsibility and the gates of the cemetery were closed. No further maintenance work was carried out, and the cemetery was left to decay and slowly return to nature.

In 1975, the present owners, the London Borough of Southwark, acquired the cemetery by Compulsory Purchase Order. Today the cemetery is managed jointly by the Council's Park Rangers in association with the Friends of Nunhead Cemetery.

Restored shell of Little's Anglican chapel 2003
Photograph by Ron Woollacott

THE BUILDINGS OF NUNHEAD CEMETERY

The cemetery has three buildings of architectural importance: the two gate lodges at the entrance from Linden Grove, and the Anglican chapel located at the top of the drive from this entrance. All listed Grade II.

The Anglican chapel fell victim to an act of arson that took place in 1974, when fire completely destroyed the interior and roof. Overnight the building was reduced to a ruin, but in spite of its condition, it still retains a sombre, formal and dramatic exterior. The structure was stabilised and made safe, thanks to a grant from the Heritage Lottery Fund in the year 2000.

In plan, the Anglican chapel comprises a large carriage porch at the front of the building and an octagonal chapel at the rear; sandwiched between the two is an antechamber, which contains an entrance hall, with two side rooms and staircases leading to the turret and vaults. The octagonal design is found in Greek, Moslem and Early Christian architecture and was originally devised as a means of supporting a round dome in a square or rectangular building. In the Nunhead chapel, however, the roof was a simple eight-sided tent-like structure, built of timber.

Below ground level is a crypt. When originally designed, the paved floor of the chapel contained an eight-foot by four-foot opening through which coffins were lowered to the vaults below.

The architect of the chapel was Thomas Little, who won the commission in an architectural competition in 1843. Although he later went on to design a number of other churches, the Nunhead Anglican chapel is probably his most significant work.

The two gate lodges were designed by James Bunstone Bunning, the architect who designed the layout of the cemetery and also designed the cast-iron gates and Portland stone classical pillars which are decorated with cast-iron inverted torches (symbolic of the extinguishing of life). The future of the ruined East Lodge is at present undecided, but FONC are actively seeking funds in order to restore it to its original condition.

Angel amidst the trees
Photograph by Nina Giebel

THE TREES OF NUNHEAD CEMETERY

The first thing that strikes the new visitor to the cemetery is the number of trees. The older part of the site has been described as 'a wood with graves in it'. It is a dramatic demonstration of the speed with which trees can seed themselves and turn a carefully landscaped cemetery into dense secondary woodland.

The original design of the Nunhead Cemetery used specimen trees, some of them exotic, to enhance the landscape and the views. These included the Italian alder, the horse chestnuts, the holm oak and the ginkgo or maidenhair tree which was planted by the Eastern Catacomb. Native trees were also used - oak, holly and the stately limes on the main avenue. The original elms have long since succumbed to Dutch elm disease, but their descendants continue to regrow from the roots. The traditional churchyard yew was also planted, and some have now reached a respectable size. The beech trees near the Figgins monument were probably field boundary markers from the original farmland rather than ornamental plantings. There are also large numbers of hawthorns, including the familiar common and Midland hawthorns but also a few specimens of the Victorian nurseryman's creation, the variable leaved hawthorn.

The majority of the trees that occupy the cemetery, however, are self-seeded. The two dominant types are the sycamore, an introduced species, and the ash, a native tree. There are also numbers of Turkey oak, which seed more readily and grow faster than the native English oak. (More details can be found in the FONC publication *Trees and Shrubs of Nunhead Cemetery* by Carol Stevenson).

Unlike the usual practice in municipal parks, dead trees are not tidied away but log-piled in the undergrowth where they provide food and shelter for innumerable invertebrates and fungi, adding to the richness and variety of the ecology in the cemetery.

A GUIDED WALK IN NUNHEAD CEMETERY

Every last Sunday in the month, the Friends of Nunhead Cemetery lead a tour which covers some of the highlights of this remarkable cemetery. Jeff Hart describes one of these walks for the benefit of those wishing for some guidance on other occasions. The map on the centre pages outlines the route and the numbers give the suggested stopping places where you can refer to the notes. The walk will take about 2 hours. Start at the flint circle a few yards inside the Linden Grove entrance.

1 From the flint circle can be admired Bunning's grand entrance to the cemetery, with its imposing Portland stone pillars and cast iron gates and symbols. The two lodges on either side once contained the Superintendent's office and were used to house the cemetery records. But the visitor's eyes will naturally be drawn up the main avenue towards the Anglican chapel, the focal point of the cemetery. The avenue is flanked by lime, or linden trees, which lend their name to the road outside the gates (Linden Grove), once known more prosaically as Cemetery Road.

On the eastern side of the avenue (left, as you face the chapel) can be seen the tall red granite obelisk of the Livesey monument. The funeral of Sir George Thomas Livesey, chairman of the South Metropolitan Gas Company, was attended by thousands of mourners - a fitting recognition for the man who provided the first free library for working men in Camberwell (now the Livesey Museum), and introduced profit-sharing and other benefits for his employees (see also the FONC publication *Nunhead Notables* by Ron Woollacott).

2 Walking past the East Lodge, surrounded by the remnants of its symbolic planting of box, laurel, holly and yew, follow the East Crescent some ten yards or so and see how already the Gothic gloom created by dense

sycamore and ivy closes around the visitor. On your right the many monuments have all but disappeared from view, whilst on the left side of the path stands a beautiful ginkgo (or maidenhair) tree rescued from the suffocating ivy and competing sycamores.

The large, flat open space behind the ginkgo is in fact the roof of the only remaining catacomb of the five which were once to be found in the cemetery. To the right of the catacomb, in line with the ginkgo, is a large flat memorial commemorating the place of re-interment of the occupants of Saint Christopher-le-Stocks crypt which made way for an extension to the Bank of England in 1867.

3   The thick undergrowth to either side of the path hides many monuments which now show the diversity of styles to be found in Nunhead. But here one particular pleasing group is worth pausing for. Commemorating families of no particular note, they nevertheless demonstrate some of the more popular styles.

On the other side of the path, notice how the larger monuments at the path's edge gradually give way to smaller, less imposing memorials receding in the distance. This is because the more expensive plots for burial were those where the monument could be readily seen by all visitors, and thus purchasers could also afford a more imposing reminder of the lives.

4   Following the path to the right, the Anglican chapel can now be observed in more detail. Its present roofless state is the result of a fire started by three youths in 1974, but its shell remains an evocative Gothic revival work of great charm. The structure was stabilised and made safe, thanks to a grant from the Heritage Lottery Fund (HLF) in the year 2000. One day, perhaps, the building can be restored to its former glory.

As the most prestigious burial area in the cemetery, some of Nunhead's finest monuments are to be found around the chapel. Henry Daniel, monumental mason responsible for so many of Nunhead's monuments, has his own family vault at the top of the main avenue on its western side, also restored in 2000 with the help of an HLF grant. The massive red granite cross to the east of the chapel commemorates Thomas Whichelow, of Bermondsey, who not only lived in Tanner Street but appropriately made his family's fortune from the tanning of leather.

5 Retracing one's steps to the east, the fine obelisk-topped vault built by William Lucey to commemorate his wife, Anne Caroline, is worthy of a few moments of contemplation. This obelisk was damaged by a fallen tree in 2002 and for some months stood with the top portion at a perilous angle, but has now been repaired. The Lucey family are typical of so many who chose to be interred at Nunhead. William worked as a humble lighterman on the Thames, eventually becoming a shipowner of some standing. Having established himself as a respectable businessman, and winning a social position; his grandson later served as aide-de-camp to King George VI during the Second World War.

6 Walking down the Slope, past the densely packed ash saplings, the Wildman/Spurrett monument is a good example of Egyptian style funerary architecture. The stone obelisk is an obvious Egyptian symbol but the stylised carving along its borders is less obviously derived from Egyptian hieroglyphs. Note also the clasped hands symbolising a husband and wife reunited in death, or in some cases the hand of the departed reaching out for the hand of God; and the method by which the lead lettering was attached to the stone.

7 Where the Slope joins the East Path, the fallen holm oak (sole survivor of the original pair) epitomises the way the landscape planning has changed. Although well past its

prime, this reclining tree is full of character, whereas in Victorian times it would undoubtedly have been removed and replaced with a younger specimen.

Near it is the Cook headstone, with its unusual design of a broken carriage-spring, symbolising the breaking of the spring of life.

8 Turning right into the Lower Cross Path, a narrow track, 100 yards along on the left, leads to the humble headstone of one of Nunhead's most prominent 'notables' - George Howell. He was leader of the Bricklayers Union and became first General Secretary of the Trades Union Congress (TUC). His funeral was attended by the leading Members of Parliament of the then infant Labour Party (see also *Nunhead Notables*).

9 Further along the Lower Cross Path, the heavily wooded areas now give way to open scrub land. Some 600 elm trees suffering from Dutch elm disease were felled in the late 1970s, many from this area, and this opened up the floor of the cemetery allowing the smaller hawthorns, dog roses and abundant grasses to flourish. These all provide food for the seed-eating birds of the cemetery, a contributing factor to why it is able to support so many different species of bird. The area is now cut on a three-year rotation plan to allow these seed-bearing plants, and the birds that feed on them, to flourish. The area to the north of the path, behind the Anglican chapel, was where the London Cemetery Company had its glasshouses and stables. Unfortunately, no trace remains today of these wooden structures. Directly behind the chapel, a monument marks the site where the human remains from the crypt of St George's church, Wells Way, Camberwell, were re-interred in 1993.

10 At the junction of four paths is one of the areas of 1914-18 war graves maintained by the Commonwealth War Graves Commission. Here lie Canadians, South

Plan not to scale

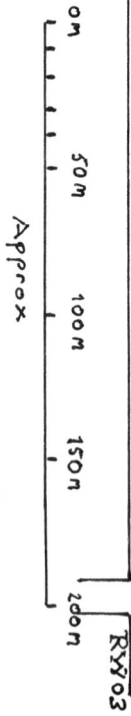

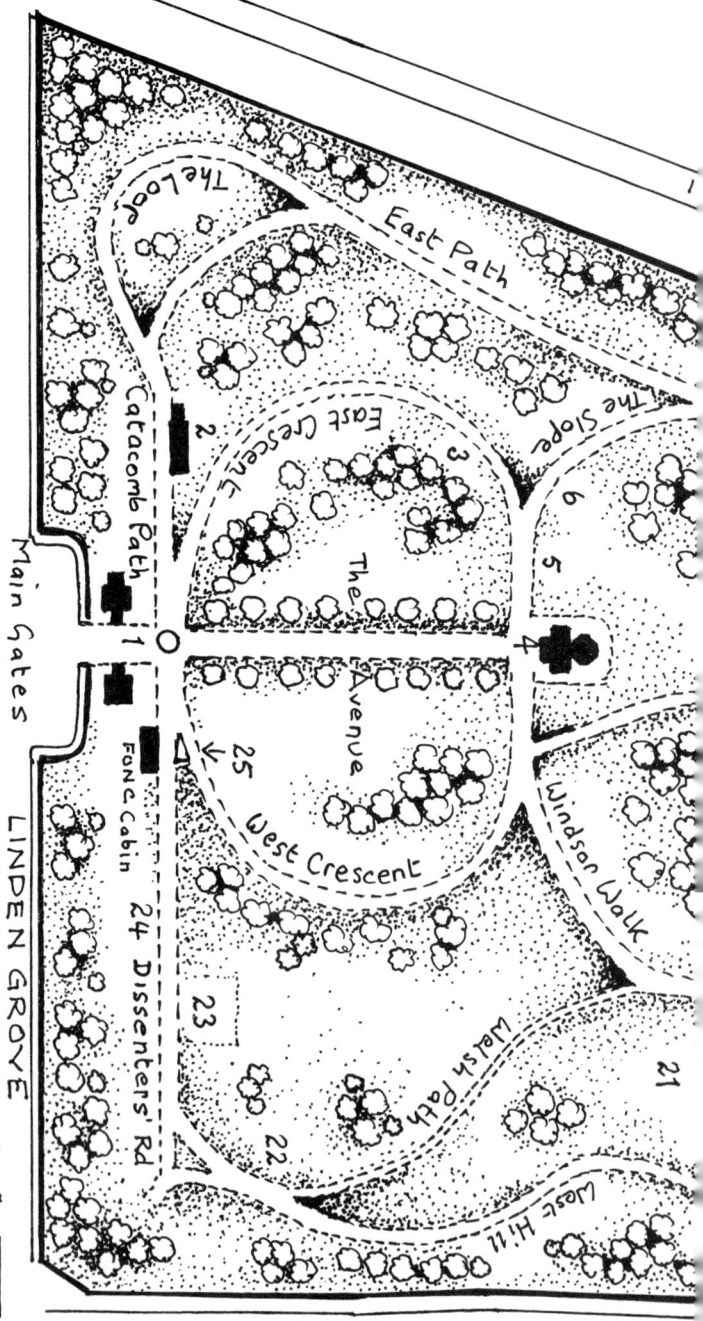

Main Gates

LINDEN GROVE

East Path

The Loop

Catacomb Path

The Slope

East Crescent

The Avenue

Windsor Walk

West Crescent

Welsh Path

Hazel Hill

Fune. Cabin

Dissenters' Rd

2

3

6

5

4

1

25

24

23

22

21

0m   50m   100m   150m   200m

Approx

RWo3

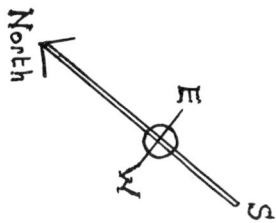

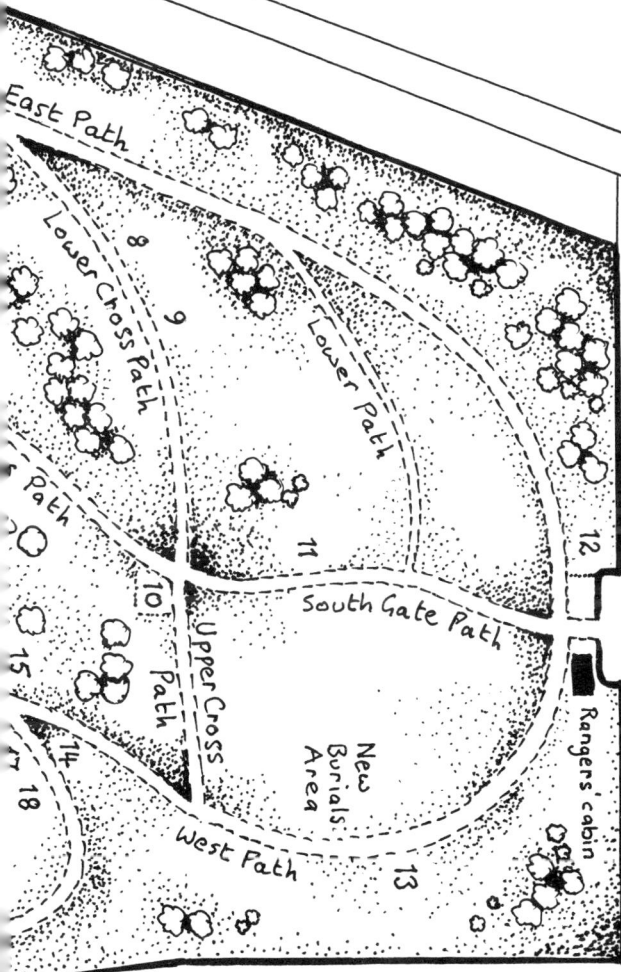

Africans, New Zealanders and a solitary Australian, presumably wounded in the great battles of France and Flanders and evacuated to to hospitals in southern England. Nearby King's College Hospital, Denmark Hill, was one of the largest such hospitals, but even their skills could not save these Empire troops. Although buried in a single plot in this case, individual war graves can be found the cemetery. Immediately to the right of this plot can be seen the 'Boy Scouts' monument, commemorating nine Scouts from Walworth who were drowned in a boating accident at the mouth of the Thames in 1912. The original monument was surmounted by a life-size bronze statue of a Scout, stolen in 1969 and presumably melted down for its scrap value. The original bronze inscription plaque disappeared at the same time but was rediscovered in a scrap yard in 2000 (as recounted in the FONC publication *The Walworth Scouts* by Rex Batten) and a replica may now be seen in the Anglican chapel.

11 Walking downhill toward the South Gate, another plot of war graves can be seen on the left, this time comprising entirely Australian war dead.

12 Just to the left of the gates, a new memorial erected in 1985/86, commemorates some 500 First World War dead and replaces an earlier memorial which was so badly vandalised that it had to be removed in the early 1970s. Adjacent to it is a commemorative wall to Second World War dead, including a number of civilians killed in bombing raids. Indeed the cemetery was itself hit on a number of occasions, particularly the north-east corner.

13 Walking up the hill along the West Path, the visitor can see the effect of the Council's current burial policy in Nunhead. At one time it was proposed to clear some 22 acres of the cemetery to provide burial space for the

Borough for a 40 year period. Continue up West Path to the junction with an avenue on your left.

14 Entering the tree canopy once again, a fine family vault, designed by the architect W P Griffith, was built in 1844 for one Vincent Figgins. He was a successful type founder - 'Figgins' Fist' is a phrase still familiar to printers today - whose son, James, continued the family business and later became MP for Shrewsbury from 1868 to 1874. Both are interred in the family vault (see *Nunhead Notables*).

15 Underneath the impressive beach trees - perhaps the only mature trees on the site which actually pre-date the cemetery itself - is the red granite vault wherein lies Sir Charles Fox. Although it is Sir Joseph Paxton who is widely remembered as the architect of the Crystal Palace, it was Fox who, together with his gang of workmen, actually constructed Paxton's fantasy of glass and ironwork in practice.

16 Retracing one's steps towards the Figgins monument, the family vaults of the Donkins can be seen on the right. Bryan Donkin the elder's chief claim to fame is his invention in 1812 of a method of preserving meat in airtight metal cans (see also *Nunhead Notables*).

17 Taking the path up the hill to the right, Nunhead's most impressive monument looms above the visitor. It is that of John Allan, whose bronze bas-relief portrait can be seen at the rear of the tomb. Based on the design of the mausoleum of Payava of Xanthos, comparatively little is known about John Allan himself, other than his Yorkshire origins and his merchant shipping connections. How sad that a monument of such magnificent proportions houses a Victorian almost forgotten today!

18 Adjacent to the Allan monument is Nunhead's only

surviving mausoleum: the overground version of the brick-built, underground family vault. This belongs to the Stearns family and was built about 1900. It is brick built, faced with terracotta tiles, and is particularly noteworthy for the Romanesque-style decoration around its entrance, which we believe is unique for a monument of this type in London.

19 Looking to the left to admire the fine views towards the North Downs in the distance, climb to the top of Nunhead Hill (200ft above sea level), where can be found some of the most impressive monuments in the cemetery. This was a particularly favoured, and expensive, area for burial plots as it was regarded as the nearest point to God. The inscription on the solid grey granite block which commemorates Thomas Wing tells its own story (see also *Nunhead Notables*) whilst the monument to its right reflects Bunning's choice of the the upturned torch motif on the main gates. The massive, rough-hewn granite obelisk commemorates William Chadwick, a typically versatile Victorian engineer who built canals, railway bridges, churches and houses (see *Nunhead Notables*). That this monument still stands perfectly erect today is a tribute to the efforts of the men (and horses) who toiled up the hill with the stone and used block and tackle to set it up.

20 From the top of the hill, St Paul's Cathedral can be seen in the distance, framed by the trees. This view was recreated during the Heritage Lottery Fund works of 2000/01; a number of trees which were felled for this have been left in situ to slowly rot. During the autumn dead wood in the cemetery is covered by thousands of fungi - over a hundred different species have been counted here. By degrading in this way the trees return the richness to the soil which led to their initial healthy growth, and so maintain the cycle of regeneration which makes the cemetery such an important ecological site.

21 Leave the main path to walk across the Wetland area to see the family vault of Schroeter and Oppenheim. The monument reflects in its bas-relief sculpture John Moritz Oppenheim's love and patronage of the Arts. Oppenheim himself is also depicted on his death-bed, his soul about to be escorted to Heaven by an angel (see also the FONC publication *More Nunhead Notables*). To the left can be seen a simple brick grave, now covered with a metal grid. Its bowed sides prevent the structure from falling in and the quality of bricklaying says a great deal about the Victorian attitude towards the burial of the dead. The Wetland area was opened up and the seasonal pond created by volunteers from the Friends of Nunhead Cemetery (with a small grant from English Nature) during the very wet winter of 1994 to 1995.

22 Returning to the main West Hill path, the steep descent of Nunhead Hill continues until it reaches, on the right hand side, the monument to Sir Polydore de Keyser. Originally from Belgium, he became the proprietor of the then famous De Keyser's Royal Hotel, Blackfriars. More importantly, however, in 1887, he was the first Roman Catholic to be elected Lord Mayor of London since Henry VIII's suppression of the monasteries in 1538. Until the Catholic Emancipation Act of 1829, all Roman Catholics were barred from holding public office in this country and, even then, anti-papist prejudice was a formidable hurdle to overcome (see also *Nunhead Notables*).

23 Following the path to the right into Dissenters' Road, the empty site of the Dissenters' chapel can be seen. It was this part of the cemetery which remained unconsecrated by the Anglican Bishop of Winchester to provide a burial place for those of a non-Anglican or 'dissenting', faith Thomas Little's building was very similar in design to the Anglican chapel which remains. Having been damaged by enemy action in the last war, it was subsequently demolished by the London Cemetery Company. Now the site forms the lower part of an area which Southwark Borough Council has cleared of monuments to form an open amenity area stretching back up the hill to the Wetland area.

24 Along the Dissenters' Road are interred many notable Baptists, Congregationalists, Wesleyan Methodists, and other nonconformists who are perhaps typified by the Reverend James Wells, a Baptist minister who was brought up in a workhouse. Self-educated, he preached at the 2,000 seat tabernacle at Wansey Street, Walworth, which he regularly filled to capacity (see *Nunhead Notables*).

25 The final highlight of the tour is, of course, the Scottish Political Martyrs monument. This was erected by public subscription raised in 1851 by the radical MP Joseph Hume, following the raising of a similar monument at Edinburgh's Calton Hill cemetery. Nunhead appears to have been chosen as a site for this second monument because the coffee houses in Southwark at the time were known as hot-beds of radical politics, and Nunhead was the nearest cemetery to Southwark. The monument commemorates five men who, having agitated for parliamentary reform in the early 1790s, at the time of the French Revolution, were transported to Australia for a period of seven years for their pains. Their story is told more fully in another FONC booklet (*The Scottish Martyrs* by Wally Macfarlane), following the publication of which the monument was refurbished by Southwark Borough Council in 1984/85.

It only remains for the visitor now to return to the starting point of the tour pausing to reflect, we hope, on the many aspects of interest that have been pointed out on this walk and, hopefully, returning on other occasions to explore the many parts of the cemetery that we have not been able to show you this time.

A group of monuments on the Slope.
The tallest obelisk belongs to the Wildman and Spurrett families (see page 14)
Photograph by Ron Woollacott

MONUMENTS AND THEIR MEANING

For much of the 19th century, tombstones for Anglicans and even more for Dissenters avoided anything that smacked of Popery. Figures of saints or angels, direct representations of Christ, the cross - all were replaced by motifs and symbols derived from classical Rome.

The majority of the early graves at Nunhead follow simple classical styles, most commonly the simple round-headed stone. The taller and more impressive forms offered in this style were the column, surmounted by a figure or a ball, and the obelisk. The association of classical styles with Protestantism accounts for the choice of an obelisk to commemorate the Scottish martyrs in a monument dated 1851.

Decorative devices tend to emphasise the fact of mortality: inverted torches to suggest life being snuffed out, cut flowers, weeping figures, broken column to show that life has been cut off. A further range of devices was based on ancient Roman funeral customs: urns (the Romans were known to have practised cremation) and funeral palls, whether draped over the urn or simply carved on the stone in isolation. Portraits or occupational emblems - such as the chrysanthemum carved on the obelisk of the noted gardener Samuel Broome - appeared on a number of stones.

The growing acquaintance with Greek architecture and monuments, culminating in the arrival in England of the Elgin marbles, led many artists to the conclusion that the long copied Roman models were inferior to their Greek originals; in order to return to this purer style, they demanded a paring down of ornament, a more austere and geometric style, lettering without Roman serifs. The Figgins tomb of 1844, by the architect W P Griffith, with its urn based on archaic Greek rather than Roman models, is a good example of this tendency. The more knowledgeable Greek revivalists could nonetheless produce complex and decorative works, as witness the Allan tomb of 1867, modelled on the Payava tomb at Xanthos which had been discovered in the 1830s.

On the other hand, the attempt to disengage oneself from

sectarian controversy often led in the second quarter of the century to the use of the Egyptian style, which had become widely familiar too recently (since Napoleon's Egyptian expedition) to have any denominational associations. The London Cemetery Company, probably in an effort to demonstrate its lack of sectarian restrictions, placed a mixture of classical, Gothic and Egyptian buildings in Nunhead and Highgate cemeteries, using Portland stone classical gate piers with cast-iron inverted torches at Nunhead.

The Gothic architects mounted an attack on the continued use of classical motifs, which they saw as pagan in origin and thus unworthy of use in a Christian country. A clear set of alternatives was recommended: pointed instead of round-headed tombstones; the cross instead of the urn; imitations of Eleanor crosses instead of obelisks; Gothic decoration and lettering; symbols that stood for immortality of the soul instead of the mortality of the body.

In the later part of the 19th century, the rail network across Britain and Europe meant that it was now possible to import stone from other areas for use in monuments. Italian marble became immediately popular, although it proved not very resistant to the English weather. By the 1880s, not only Italian marble but marble figures carved by masons in Italy were available for use in England, and virtually all full-figure angels have been thus imported - the English mason's job being to carve the pedestal and inscription.

The 1890s saw the appearance of the Celtic cross, in which the arms are connected to form a wheel. The popularity of this form seems at first to have been connected with the Celtic revival in arts, rather than its antiquity as the earliest surviving form of native Christian art; the shaft of the Celtic cross could be filled either with attempts at genuine Celtic-style interlacing, or with simple floral patterns.

The First World War saw a massive campaign to provide fitting graves for all the soldiers who had been killed, and the Imperial (now Commonwealth) War Graves Commission, with the architects Lutyens and Blomfield (the latter the designer of the cross with the superimposed sword) as advisers, quickly decided to eliminate invidious distinctions of rank by adopting a uniform design for all its headstones. The Commission maintains two small plots in Nunhead, in which this pattern can be seen.

The most recent trend at Nunhead, to be seen in the new burials area, is the move to the lawn cemetery, in which headstones only are erected, without kerbs or other devices which would interrupt the smooth swathe of turf and get in the way of the lawn mower. Ease of maintenance has today replaced the grave owner's taste as the prime determinant of monumental style.

A group of monuments along the Dissenters' Road
Photograph by Ron Woollacott

FLOWERS OF NUNHEAD CEMETERY

The wide assortment of flora in Nunhead reflects the changing face of the cemetery over the years. The original formal planting on graves has spread to mix with wild meadow flowers, whilst the shadier conditions, where trees have multiplied and shrub thickened, promotes the growth of plants more readily associated with true woodland habitat than an urban cemetery.

The abundant ivy keeps the cemetery green in winter and shady in summer. In January, winter heliotrope sends up its spurs of pale mauve flowers and carpets of snowdrops spread amongst the gravestones. These bulbs have naturalised and multiplied together with daffodils and bluebells, which can be glimpsed through the boundary fence along Linden Grove.

The long grass is full of early wild flowers such as cow parsley, garlic mustard, lesser stitchwort and ground ivy. More delicate early flowers include primrose, forget-me-not and wood anemone, the latter's small white flowers being seen sprinkling the banks opposite the large beeches by the Figgins monument.

Along the West Crescent, dog's mercury grows - a species associated with ancient woodland when seen growing on clay soil. Other plants are valuable in supplying food for butterflies such as the meadow brown and speckled wood, the latter feeding on cocksfoot grass and the gardener's nightmare - couch grass. The red and white dead nettles and the stinging nettle both have their value in attracting the colourful peacock, tortoiseshell and comma butterflies. In summer the glades and pathways are alive with bees and butterflies, particularly around the buddleia or aptly named 'butterfly bush' (see FONC booklet *The Butterflies of Nunhead Cemetery* by Richard A Jones).

Other plants which provide food for humans grow throughout the cemetery. Chickweed and dandelion leaves can be used in salad, ground elder and fat hen can be cooked like spinach, and the large glossy-leaved horseradish's grated root is used to garnish many a Sunday dinner. Sorrel is esteemed as an ingredient of salads and sauces.

Amongst the bramble, hawthorn and elder that edge many paths, various climbing plants can be observed. Probably the favourite of many are the wild roses that make the green paths so attractive in summer with their blooms and in autumn with their red hips. Climbing on and around these are greater bindweed, honeysuckle, bush vetch and one which is often inadvertently taken home with you, goose grass, whose stems, leaves and fruit have hooked bristles that catch on clothing. More apparent in late summer and early autumn are the red berries of the purple flowering woody nightshade and the distinctive fluffy silvery fruits of the wild clematis which gives it the descriptive title of 'old man's beard'.

Some of Nunhead's many wild flowers drawn by Maggie Hart

Along the sunnier path borders and in the less densely wooded areas, assorted meadow flowers are sprinkled throughout the grass. Amongst these are buttercups, ox eye daisy, field poppy and clover. Larger splashes of colour are provided in places by cultivated flowers that have run wild - lupin, golden rod, saxifrage and Michaelmas daisy continue to thrive.

GRAVE SEARCH AND GENEALOGY

The records for burials in Nunhead Cemetery are comprehensive as far back as 1840, the date of opening. They are in the care of *Southwark Council Bereavement Services, Camberwell New Cemetery, Brenchley Gardens, LONDON, SE23 3RD.* To obtain the details, you will need to know the full name of the deceased and date of death or number of the grave.

Monumental Inscriptions (MIs) often provide more information than can be found in burial registers. Transcripts of MIs from some cleared burial grounds will be found in the Public Record Office (PRO). The Society of Genealogists has a growing collection of MIs, as does FONC.

Useful addresses

Records of births, deaths and marriages registered in England and Wales since 1837 are kept at:

> The Family Records Centre
> 1 Myddleton Street
> LONDON
> EC1R 1UR

For genealogical research:

> Society of Genealogists
> 14 Charterhouse Buildings
> LONDON
> EC1M 7BA

FRIENDS OF NUNHEAD CEMETERY (FONC)

FONC was awarded HM Queen Elizabeth the Queen Mother's
Birthday Award for Environmental Improvements
(National Commendation) in 1998

Formed in 1981, FONC is a registered charity number 296413,
an independent non party-political voluntary group, and a
founder member of the National Federation of Cemetery
Friends. It exists to represent all those with an interest in the
cemetery. The group seeks to promote the conservation and
appreciation of the cemetery as a place of remembrance, of
historical importance and of natural beauty.

Members receive *FONC News*, a quarterly journal, and
occasional talks, guided visits and other events are arranged.
There is a conducted tour of the cemetery, open to all and free
of charge, on the last Sunday of every month. It starts from the
Linden Grove gates at 2.15pm and lasts about 2 hours.

We carry out practical conservation work in the cemetery on
the first Sunday of each month starting at 10.00am. All
volunteers are welcome. Stay an hour or two or all day - it's up
to you. We also do monumental inscription recording, and
again, volunteers are welcome. Dates are shown on the notice
boards by the cemetery gates and in *FONC News*.

Additional information about the Friends of Nunhead Cemetery
and all FONC's publications, including those referred to in this
guidebook, will be found on our website at **www.fonc.org.com**

**The cemetery is open from 8.30am to 4.00pm daily and
stays open later during the spring and summer months.**

For further information, please contact *Ron Woollacott, FONC
Chairman, 185 Gordon Road, LONDON, SE15 3RT*

If you would like to join FONC, please contact *Simon Mercer,
Membership Secretary - telephone 020-8452 5239*